A Marine of Imperial Guard: Eyewitness to the French Failure in Spain, 1808

Recollections of Admiral, General, and Count Pierre de Baste

Tim Mahon

NIMBLE BOOKS LLC

TIM MAHON

ISBN-13: 978-1-934840-50-4

ISBN-10: 1-934840-50-5

Copyright 2008 Tim Mahon

Version 1.0; last saved 2009-08-20.

Nimble Books LLC

1521 Martha Avenue

Ann Arbor, MI 48103-5333

http://www.nimblebooks.com

Contents (including Figures)

TIM MAHON

FOREWORD

The Napoleonic period abounds with memoirs, recollections and autobiographies of officers, soldiers and seamen from most of the nations embroiled in what might arguably be termed the first world war, especially from Great Britain and France. Some of the latter, written by men whose deeds or characters have won them the recognition of posterity, have been translated into English, sometimes in several versions, and are more or less easily available today. However, there are hundreds of memoirs lying undisturbed in libraries and private archives throughout France that have never been made available in the English language. Many of them have languished in obscurity since their first publication in the nineteenth century.

When conducting research into sources for a book on the Andalusian campaign of 1808—the first occasion on which one of Napoleon's armies capitulated and one which sent a clarion call round Europe that the Corsican Ogre was not, in fact, invincible—I found one of these memoirs. As I delved into it, it became apparent that here was an extraordinary memoir; one that was as critical of the strategy and tactics of the campaign's French commander as it was bombastic and self-serving in the interests of the author. On finishing an initial reading, I determined to translate it for research purposes, which later transformed into an ambition to publish it for a wider audience. An earlier version of this translation won an Honourable Mention in the Napoleon Series' Annual Writing

Competition in 2006, in the category of *Best Publication and/or Translation into English of New Archival Material or Books Long Out of Print,* since when it has been amended and clarified where needed. The Napoleon Series is strongly recommended to serious and not-so-serious students of the Napoleonic period alike—it is the largest site of its kind on the Internet and can be found at www.napoleon-series.org. Pierre Baste, who ended his life in combat as a General of Brigade and a Count of the Empire of the French at the age of 46, was born to humble origins in Bordeaux in 1768. His early career in the merchant marine and the navy of the French Republic are not recorded in any great detail, other than that which appears at the beginning of this memoir. The principal interest of these "Recollections" is in the detailed narrative and analysis of the campaign and eventual capitulation of Baílen in Andalusia, June-July 1808.

Although sometimes bombastic and self-aggrandizing, Baste comes across as an informed commentator on the Baílen campaign. While he is frequently critical of General Dupont's indecision and deployment at both the strategic and tactical levels—both of which were sometimes "evidently contrary to the principles of war," in Baste's own words—he also demonstrates an appreciation of the difficult position in which Dupont found himself through a combination of unfortunate circumstances. With a corps consisting largely of new recruits with minimal training, led by an officer corps drawn from depots and newly-commissioned lieutenants, living off the countryside in a region barely able to support its own population and marching hither and yon in a summer of extraordinary heat, it is doubtful whether any other of Napoleon's aspiring generals would have done any better, given the same intelligence and countermanded orders that were Dupont's lot.

Baste saw both sides of the principal argument that raged at Baílen—whether Vedel's division should be included in the capitulation or not—since he shuttled between Dupont's headquarters and that of Vedel throughout the day. He also throws considerable light onto ancillary actions of the campaign, including the action at the bridge at Alcolea, the sack of Cordoba and the pacification of Jaen, in all of which he was personally involved. For these reasons, despite the occasional tendency towards exaggeration of the importance of his own role, his memoir is an important contribution to the study of the Andalusian campaign. It would be a poor historian who ignored this eyewitness account. In this translation I have struggled to provide the sense of what Baste is trying to convey, rather than a literal translation of phrases that may be anachronistic, no longer in popular usage or misleading. There are thus particular passages that a professional translator may take issue with—but I believe I succeed in staying true to the original intent of the author throughout the 18,000 words of his text. The reader should be aware of the conventions I have adopted. All ranks and peculiarly French expressions, for which there is either no direct English equivalent or for which a broad acceptance of the French original is held by English readers, are maintained in the original French and *italicised*. Footnotes consist of translations of the footnotes of the original editors/publishers of the Baste text, except where explanatory notes have been inserted by me—these are prefixed with the title of "Translator's note" in order to distinguish them.

INTRODUCTION

This memoir provides an eyewitness account of several of the actions of the 1808 Andalusian campaign, culminating in the battle of Bailén and the capitulation of Dupont's entire army. Very little material has hitherto been available in English dealing with this campaign—thus the reader can expect to discover fresh details and new insights not available in the general histories of the Peninsular War.

ABOUT THE AUTHOR

Tim Mahon has had a career in the defense and aerospace industries spanning three decades, including fifteen years with Jane's Information Group and ten years in the United States. Since 2001 he has been a freelance journalist and business consultant based in Cheltenham, 100 miles west of London. He specialises in issues of military technology and defense business development, and acts as European Correspondent for _Training & Simulation Journal_ and _C4ISR Journal_. His interest in Napoleonic history has verged on the obsessive for more than 30 years.

TIM MAHON

ACKNOWLEDGEMENTS

Any book—even a translation—is a result of a collaborative effort. I freely acknowledge the assistance happily given by colleagues on the Napoleonic Series discussion forum over several years, which have helped my understanding of the period to the point at which I dare interpret a memoir such as this. The errors and misinterpretations, if they exist, remain my sole responsibility.

Any book is also indebted to its publisher for having the faith to invest the time and resources to bring the work to the public. In this respect, I am very grateful to Fred Zimmerman of Nimble Books, LLC, for the faith and interest he had in this idea from day one.

Finally, this book is for my parents, Brian Boru and Hazel Gloria Mahon, who gave me the gift of a love of history at a frighteningly early age.

THE RECOLLECTIONS OF *CAPITAINE DE FREGATE* PIERRE BASTE[1]

Commander of the 3rd company of the battalion of the Marins de la Garde Impériale[2], forming a part of the army of lieutenant-général Dupont, in Andalusia, during the months of May, June, July and August 1808.

Originally published in French in Beauchamp, Alphonse de, Collection des mémoires relatifs aux Révolutions d'Espagne, *Michaud, Paris, 1824*

TRANSLATED FROM THE FRENCH AND ANNOTATED BY TIM MAHON

I cannot start these memoirs, which were never intended to see the light of day, without saying who I am; without making known how, through my conduct and several notable feats, I gained senior rank in both the navy and the army. I confess that it was after having attracted the attention and the approval of the Emperor Napoleon, so great an appreciator of men and events; yet I never hid the

---

[1] At the beginning and end of these recollections can be found the complete biography of capitaine Baste, made general in 1813 and killed at the battle of Brienne in 1814.

[2] *Translator's note:* Although the word *Marins* translates to "seamen," rather than 'marines', the usual translation of the title of this corps elsewhere in Napoleonic literature has been Marines. In order to avoid a descent into argument over semantic trivia, I have elected to maintain the French title of this unit throughout this translation.

1

truth from him; I always spoke to him frankly, sometimes even with the coarseness characteristic of an admirer and imitator of Jean-Bart.[3] He always listened to me, sometimes with a little humour or impatience; but he always understood I would serve him to my last gasp, with the same devotion and the same constancy. He was right; I am devoted to him in life and to the death.

I was born in Bordeaux on 21st November 1768, the son of Jacques Baste and Marguerite Sol, a woman of exemplary virtue and conduct. My father, employed variously in the armaments industry during the war in America, had a comfortable living, and he steered me in the direction of a naval career at an early age. I first went to sea in the merchant marine on 12th July 1781, at the age of 13. It took me ten years to complete my maritime education. Should I have the time one day to undertake a thorough publication of my recollections and diaries, I will go into the curious details of my first sea voyages and the surprising adventures which, during both peace and war, marked my every step. Limited here to an exact and factual account, I must not overstep the boundaries I have laid down for myself.

I can say without digressing that, being an enthusiastic supporter of the Revolution, I threw myself headlong into the career that awaited the adventurous. I was named *enseigne auxiliaire* in 1793, and *capitaine* in 1794. In my first

---

[3] *Translator's note*: A reference to Jean Bart (1650-1702), a legendary corsair and the most famous son of the town of Dunkerque, where the 'sons of Jean Bart' are still a central feature of the annual carnival.

campaign I commanded the schooner *Hirondelle* in Santo Domingo and the following year the brig *Jacobin*, tasked with exploring the coastline of New England. Having distinguished myself in combat on 5 *messidor an III*[4] and again on 2 *frimaire an IV*[5], I found myself in the Lake Garda flotilla, in command of the galley *Voltigeuse*. I went from there to the lakes of Mantua where I took part in several engagements with honour and ended by commanding the national flotilla during the siege and blockade. There I came to the attention of General Bonaparte. On the recommendation of Generals Andréossi and Serrurier, having never ceased to display my diligence, bravery and intelligence during the siege and blockade of Mantua, Bonaparte cleared the way for my advancement. This is how General Serrurier expressed himself: "I could not be more satisfied with the conduct that *lieutenant de vaisseau* Baste has displayed during the blockade of Mantua, on the lake on which he commands a squadron. I sent a report at the time to General Bonaparte who undertook to solicit his well-deserved advancement. I will do everything possible to achieve this for him and to prove to him the confidence I have in him." I had been made *enseigne de vaisseau* on 21st March 1796; I then obtained a brevet commission to *lieutenant de marine*. From 1797 to 1798 I commanded the 18 gun brig *Mérope*.

---

[4] *Translator's note*: 23rd June 1795.
[5] *Translator's note*: 23rd November 1795.

Having been part of the expedition to Egypt, I was at Aboukir during the fighting on *16 thermidor an VI*[6]. I was then deployed to the siege of Malta, where I had command of Gunboat No. 1. A short time thereafter I captained the felucca *Légère* in the Mediterranean. Tasked with delivering despatches to the governor of Malta in the month of *floréal an VIII*[7], the city being very closely blockaded, I squeezed through under the enemy's guns and returned to Toulon having executed the orders I had been given and having avoided detection and pursuit by the blockading cruisers a second time. My ship having no decks, and offering, therefore, but little shelter from the sea, all the effects I had taken aboard with me were completely ruined. The Minister of the Marine requested compensation for me, which was duly granted. Returning to Malta, I was tasked by *contre-amiral* Villeneuve with fulfilling the terms of the articles of capitulation, and with taking command of the seamen who remained there. On *1 vendémaire an VIII*[8] *contre-amiral* Villeneuve and General Vaubois attested that I had penetrated as far as Gozo, commanding a gunboat, despite the crossfire from the enemy batteries, resulting in my learning the situation of the weak garrison there, and that I contributed to a sturdy defence of Chambray fort, whose garrison I took back to Malta.

I also drew the attention of the Ricazoli fort, where I commanded a detachment of sailors, to myself. The courage

---

[6] *Translator's note:* 3rd August 1798.
[7] *Translator's note:* April-May 1800.
[8] *Translator's note:* 23rd September 1799.

and industry I displayed was of considerable utility and contributed to the preservation of a large part of the garrison.

On 17th May 1800 General Bonaparte, having become First Consul, confirmed my brevet as *lieutenant de vaisseau* and I became part of the ill-fated Santo Domingo expedition, whose outcome I foretold and in which I should have died twice; first during the second fire at Cape Town, which I endeavoured in vain to prevent in daring to offer myself twice to Saint Christopher, and later by a bout of illness. Finally, on my return, I was promoted *capitaine de frégate* on 20 September 1803, the close of the year being marked for me by an enormous favour that decided my military career. I was appointed commander of the 3rd *équipage* of the battalion of *Marins de la Garde.*[9] I was soon deployed to the fleet at Boulogne, and on the coastline at Le Havre. I had the good fortune to distinguish myself at the mouth of the Seine on *14 thermidor an XII*[10], the day on which fourteen English vessels, including two ships of the line, bombarded the town of Le Havre and the squadron of vessels moored in the harbour and at the quayside to defend the town. I embarked on Gunboat No. 151, the *Bolonaise*, and fought at close quarters with an English cutter and a brig: I dismasted the brig of its main topmast and I forced them both make themselves scarce. In this case I well deserved the praise of my superiors and the population of Le Havre. Napoleon, informed of the action I had been in,

---

[9] *Translator's note:* This was the Consular Guard at the time.
[10] *Translator's note:* 2nd August 1804.

made a very flattering report on my behalf, which appeared in the papers and which Admiral Bruix included in the order of the day to the fleet.

I was later detached to Ostend, where I served under *contre-amiral* Magon, to activate the port's defences. I distinguished myself again at Calais and at Dunkirk; there I was praised by Marshal Soult for my bravery and conduct during the various combats I was involved in round the ports of Calais and Boulogne. Few seamen had gained as much experience as I had in navigating the areas around both our coasts. With the Emperor I took part in the celebrated 1806 campaign in Austria, where I rendered service on the Danube, in the port of Vienna and on the island of Lobau, that was not exactly stunning but was nonetheless appreciated. In 1807 I was again detached to the *Grande Armée*, where I put together a flotilla at Danzig to support operations against Pillau. There I seized a convoy of 42 sail carrying supplies to the enemy. At the conclusion of this glorious campaign, which culminated in the Battle of Friedland and peace, I was detached to the Army of Spain, at the beginning of 1808.

It is the regrettable Andalusian campaign, to which I was close enough to be able to judge the mistakes and follow the ups and downs, of which I plan to write in detail. Of all the feats of arms in which I have been involved, this is the one, without a doubt, that had the greatest effect on me and about which public curiosity has been the strongest.

I have decided and so will now begin my account.

The first columns of the Second Corps, under the command of *lieutenant-général* Dupont, arrived at Irun on 25th November 1807, and continued their advance towards Vittoria; everywhere the officers and men were made perfectly welcome by the Spaniards; the behaviour of the authorities and the populace at large was at first very friendly. The corps entered Burgos and then occupied Valladolid; Dupont arrived there on 20th January and there reviewed the troops, which were not yet completely organized.

It was at Valladolid that I rejoined the army with the battalion of *Marins de la Garde Impériale*, commanded by *capitaine de vaisseau* Daugier, and of which I was the second in command. The fact that the *Marins de la Garde* were joined with an army corps that was thus strengthened to some 30,000 began to make us suspect that our destination was to be Cadiz, where we knew a naval squadron lay at anchor. In fact, General Dupont was charged with entering Cadiz and taking possession of the Spanish fleet there, as welll as the vessels moored at Cueta and Oran. It was therefore obvious what was to be the destination of the *Marins de la Garde*.

General Dupont's corps, encamped at Valladolid, Zamora and other towns along the right bank of the Douro, was composed of the following units after its final organisation: two divisions of infantry commanded by Generals Rouyer and Barbou; a division of cavalry under the orders of *lieutenant-général* Baron Frésia—a Piedmontese officer strongly devoted to France and the Emperor; a detachment of the gendarmerie; the *Marins de la Garde*, scarcely a thousand men under arms, and finally a proportionate artillery park, commanded by General Faultrier.

At Valladolid we learned that Marshal Moncey was organising a new army corps at Burgos and that Marshal Berthier was gathering a third at Bayonne. We began to suspect that the Emperor had not sought passage for these troops solely for Portugal and in fact intended to establish them in Spain. Everything led us to believe the Spanish were not becoming alarmed without reason. The aristocracy and the clergy, however, did not see everything in as black a light as the populace, since they had confidence in Napoleon, who was then greatly revered throughout Spain.

The weather was so good in mid-February that it resembled an early May in France; we thus occupied the troops in large-scale exercises. They had great need of training since, with the exception of several battalions of the *Garde de Paris* and a Swiss regiment, the troops consisted almost totally of conscripts raised during the winter of 1807, scarcely broken in at the depots of the regiments to which they had been attached and badly dressed and equipped. As for the officers, the greater part of them had been recalled to duty after a long period of inactivity, or had come direct from military colleges. They were all brave and full of good will; but they lacked the necessary experience of those who pursue the profession of arms.

However, the successive entry of French troops and their distribution among different towns had already exacerbated Spanish discontent. In the provinces, towards the end of February, one could already see that Madrid was home to serious trouble, and that an explosion appeared imminent. A general outcry against the Prince of Peace[11] began to be heard. Unrest and agitation began to reach their heights in early March. By mid-March General Dupont's corps consisted of some 18,000 men all told. It had exercised well at Valladolid, where the conscripts were already manoeuvring as well as the more seasoned troops. On 13th March, during a firing exercise, *général de division* Maller was killed by a ramrod that penetrated his skull—his loss was greatly regretted. The same evening the entire corps received orders to march for Madrid in three divisions by three different routes.

The headquarters reached Guadarama on 20th March, at the foot of the mountains near Madrid and some seven leagues from the capital. We were billeted with the populace in the surrounding villages, where we formed our grenadier companies into battalions, which did much to convince us of the imminence of action. These indications nonetheless came as a shock to the greater part of the officers and men. On 25th March the entire corps was encamped just two leagues from Madrid. There we became

---

[11] *Translator's note*: A reference to Manuel Godoy y Alvarez de Faria (1767-1851), principal advisor to King Charles IV, and the power behind the throne.

aware of the events at Aranjuez[12], where the aristocracy and more than 10,000 peasants had come together. The change of regime by virtue of an insurrection was a sign to us of trouble—and of war.

The Grand Duke of Berg[13] had been in Madrid since 23rd March; the new King, Ferdinand VII, entered on 24th. The drunkenness and general happiness of the Spaniards left us in no doubt as to the popularity of the King or the precarious position of the French. Nevertheless, cordial relations continued between the officers of the two nations.

I went frequently into Madrid and noted, among the social circles of the city, a great disquiet regarding our hostile attitude and the conduct of the Grand Duke of Berg. This unrest—in Madrid and in the provinces—was at its height when we learned that General Savary[14] had forced Ferdinand across the frontier. This abuse of the rights of men and of nations incensed the Spanish, who moved suddenly—with respect to us—from being polite and benevolent to being arrogant and menacing. French soldiers were murdered in small groups; the people became

---

[12] *Translator's note*: A reference to the popular uprising in reaction to the Napoleon-inspired coup d'etat in which Chalres IV was forced to abdicate in favour of his son, Ferdinand VII.
[13] *Translator's note*: Marshal Joachim Murat (1767-1815), Napoleon's brother-in-law, had been made Grand Duke of Berg in 1806, when Napoleon organised the Confederation of the Rhine. At this point in 1808 he was commander of French forces in Spain.
[14] *Translator's note*: Anne Jean Marie René Savary, created Duke of Rovigo in 1808—Murat's chief of staff at this point.

embittered; the Spaniards guarded their rights jealously; the French showed themselves similarly proprietary regarding their tradition of arms; from this developed a mutual animosity that ferocity alone would bring to a conclusion.

On 27th April, towards 10am, a peasant, leaving the church of San Francesco de Madrid, felt moved by the Blessed Virgin (according to his own testimony) to kill the first three Frenchmen he came across, and to incite a revolt in the capital. The first two Frenchmen this fanatic saw were in a grocer's shop. He attacked them with an enormous cutlass. Wounding one of them—a drummer—with a violent blow to the stomach, and killing the other, he fulfilled his supposedly divine quest against a lieutenant of the 16th Line Infantry, whom he brought to his knees with a mortal blow. The fanatic was captured and shot. Such was the sad prelude to the massacres of 2nd May and the general uprising that heralded the revolution in Spain.

I do not intend to unveil the drama of the massacres of 2nd May here; this I will leave to more able raconteurs. Besides—I was not actually in Madrid on the fatal day—I heard nothing except the canon-fire and musketry.

In general, the officers—being on the whole better informed and more clear-sighted—viewed the turn of events in Spanish affairs with sadness. But their loyalty to the Emperor, and the military élan which the French never abandoned, caused us in general to carry out the orders we were given in a precise and faithful manner.

The Second Corps left the heights around Madrid for Andalusia on 22nd May. The commanding general[15] had just established himself in the region round Toledo, with the 1st infantry and the cavalry divisions. He maintained his headquarters there until he received, at the end of May, orders from the Grand Duke of Berg to march on Cadiz. *Lieutenant-général* Vedel received an order at the same time to move to replace us at Toledo. We marched off towards the town of Manzanarès. Everywhere en route we found evidence—in the general demeanour of the Spanish people—of the unfortunate perceptions that had led to the fatal confrontation of 2nd May. Individually, our security was compromised; to avoid ambush and assassination we had to march closed up in column. Stragglers and thieves were inevitably massacred.

Destined for Cadiz, we crossed La Mancha and the Sierra Morena—a pass that Spaniards regard as the key to Andalusia. The division passed through Mora, Madrigalejos and Villaharta to arrive at Manzanarès, which we left almost immediately. Our order of march on leaving this town should suffice to clarify the reality of our situation. We marched in brigade formation, with scouts deployed as if we were surrounded by the enemy. On 27th May we arrived at Valdepeñas, where the famous wine of La Mancha is produced. On 28th May we passed through Santa-Crux and rested at Elviso, a village on the right side of the Sierra Morena gorges. On 29th we passed through the

---

[15] *Translator's note*: Baste frequently uses this epithet to refer to General Dupont.

famous gorge, of which the Spanish had been telling us so much ever since we left Madrid, and rested at La Carolina, a charming town populated by Germans who had founded it some 44 years before. We left about 100 sick in this burg—the first of Andalusia. On 30th May we arrived at Bailen, where we left another score of sick and injured. And on 31st, finally, we arrived at Andujar on the Guadalquivir, where we camped. The fact that practically all the inhabitants of this large town had left confirmed my appreciation of the situation we were in, that we were certainly on the verge of an event that would lead—one way or another—to a declaration of war. Some of the inhabitants remaining at Andujar told us that about 25-30,000 Spaniards had assembled behind the bridge at Alcolea, about two leagues this side of Cordoba on the Guadalquivir. This news was quickly confirmed by reconnaissance patrols sent out by General Privé, commander of the advance guard. The commanding general soon learned that the whole of Andalusia had risen up; that a junta had just been formed at Seville; that bodies of rebels were forming in every part of the province, combining with regular troops at the camp of Saint Roque before Gibraltar and with those of General Solano, the Marquis of Sorroco, recently recalled from Portugal. The militia regiments of the southern provinces were also being combined with regular troops, so a *levée en masse* was in effect. The commanding general reported all these circumstances to the Grand Duke of Berg, explaining the critical position he found himself in and informing him that he intended to continue his march and to move on Cadiz. The troops that had till now marched by brigade

13

and in several columns to facilitate foraging were reunited at Andujar. General Dupont, having been informed that a considerable body of the enemy army had taken up position at the bridge at Alcolea in order to dispute his passage, pushed forward on 6th June and took position at El Carpio, where he awaited the arrival of the rest of his forces. At dawn the following day the French appeared before the bridge at Alcolea, situated at the edge of a plain, coming from the direction of Madrid. The bridge was protected by a small hill, surrounded by fairly pronounced hillocks, on which the Spanish had established a battery of 10 or 12 twelve pounders, which could sweep the plain where we were drawn up in order of battle. Echavari, the Spanish general commanding the insurgents, had also raised earthworks; these were defended by 3,000 infantry and 600 peasants, entrenched behind a *demi-lune* that encompassed the bridgehead, whose ditches were 10-12 feet deep and at least as wide. The remainder of the insurgent force, composed partially of peasants, were at some distance from the bridge.

At 11pm Barbou's division set off, the *Garde de Paris* in the van. Scouting was conducted by *voltigeurs*, by some *chasseurs à cheval* and by a company of the *Marins de la Garde*, which I commanded. At 4am on 7th June we encountered some advanced posts of the Spanish cavalry, which quickly fell back to the other side of the bridge. It was barely 5am when the entire division was deployed in front of the enemy. The weather was magnificent and promised a day of extreme heat. Having deployed his forces and placed the artillery in battery on a small hill, the commanding general sent orders to the *voltigeurs* and the *Marins de la Garde* to establish themselves on both sides of the bridge along the river, which here was about the same width as the Seine. The enemy, protected by the battery that dominated the bridge and the plain, also had the immense advantage of having two battalions of line infantry lying in wait to the left and right of the bridge, along the river in olive groves, bordered by very thick hedges, whereas we had yet to discover them. They had a further two battalions behind the bridge, quite apart from the insurgents who manned the trenches. Despite the brisk musketry, I managed to establish a small number of *Marins de la Garde*, supported by *voltigeurs*, beneath the bridge, wishing to reassure myself it had not been mined and with the additional intention of flushing out the peasants who were covered by the breastwork. Having assured myself of the solidity of the bridge, I sent my report to the commanding general, who sent one of his *aides-de-camp* to determine how the bridge could be taken. We had already been exchanging fire on all sides for nearly an hour when the general ordered the *Garde de Paris*, then commanded by *major* Estève, to take the bridge by escalade. General Pannetier's brigade, which formed part of the advance guard, advanced at the charge in order to take the bridge, while General Barbou organised additional attack columns of his own.

Alerted by the *voltigeurs* to the fact that the regiment was approaching in column, I climbed the bank of the river, followed by several of my soldiers, in order to enter the trenches at the same moment that our troops would arrive,

their muskets at the ready. We were already some 15-20
paces from the earthworks when the Spaniards opened fire
and left us with about 100-120 casualties. Only a few of my
men were struck—undoubtedly due to the impetuosity
with which they threw themselves at the barricades, each
helping the other to climb up; the net result was that
within 6-8 minutes we found ourselves on the bridge—25-
30 troops from the *voltigeurs*, the *Garde de Paris* and the
Marins de la Garde, with seven officers and a colour. We
tore along immediately—bayonets to the fore—and fell on
the Spaniards who still held to the side of the bridge; we
should have inevitably been overcome were it not for the
fact we were followed, after an interval of two minutes, by
a group of 60 soldiers whose numbers grew with every
passing second, and had we not been given covering fire by
the 3rd *Légion*[16], drawn up in line of battle to left and right of
the bridge. In less than a quarter of an hour the first
attacking column had not only the bridge in its power, but
also the buildings on the other side as well as the position
where the enemy battery was. All the peasants found in the
trenches were massacred; we pursued the Spaniards for half
an hour and came to a halt only half a league beyond the
bridge on the Cordoba road, to wait there for the rest of the
division, which took position on the olive-crowned heights.

---

[16] *Translator's note*: Baste refers often to various *Légions*—these are
the variously numbered *Légions de Réserve* which made up the
bulk of the infantry in Dupont's corps. They consisted of raw
recruits called up during the winter of 1807 and had received little
training beyond the most basic prior to entering Spain.

During the combat, the enemy had sought to take advantage of the confusion caused by our attacking columns and to cross the Guadalquivir—about a quarter league from the bridge—with a force of 2,000 cavalry, charged with surprising our baggage train and attacking the division from the rear. General Frésia immediately detached the dragoon brigade under the command of General Privé, who vigorously attacked the Spanish cavalry, putting it to the sword and to flight.

The commanding general, now master of the village of Alcolea, transferred all his troops to the right bank of the Guadalquivir and immediately set off in pursuit of the main body of the enemy, which had taken up position in front of Cordoba.

The combat at Alcolea, which might be said to open the fateful war in Spain[17], cost 140 casualties at the most in Barbou's division, which alone had undertaken the attack. The *Garde de Paris* suffered the greatest loss—amounting to 120 men, as many of whom were killed as wounded. The enemy's losses were less than ours, since they had been entrenched and since we had been unable to reach their regular troops on the other side of the bridge. There had been none there but peasants who, resisting obstinately

---

[17] *Translator's note*: Baste could not have known that the opening shots of the Peninsular War had, in fact, taken place three days earlier, between General Schwartz's Swiss and Italian troops from General Duhesme's corps and a group of local *somatenes* (Home Guard), at El Bruch Pass in southern Catalonia. A Spanish victory over the French, this small success ignited fires of patriotic fervour throughout Catalonia.

from within the houses, had been put to flight at the point of the sword.

General Dupont, having transferred all his troops to the right bank of the river, attended to the defence of the village and bridge of Alcolea; he established the battalion of the *Marins de la Garde* there, who, by virtue of their discipline and their appearance, inspired the greatest confidence. I asked for and was given permission to join the general staff, there to be employed as necessary in the form of a volunteer for the more hazardous duties. I placed myself with the advanced guard in pursuit of the Spaniards who had just been defeated, who were hastening to join the bulk of their army. This army had taken up position before Cordoba, capital city of the kingdom of the same name. It was about 10am when we noticed on our right a body of enemy cavalry observing us. We pursued them till we came in sight of Cordoba, but without bringing them to any action. We took several prisoners and learned that the advanced guard of the Spanish insurrection forces, part of which we had just defeated at Alcolea, were commanded by General Don Pedra Augustino Eschavari (sic) and that he had some regular troops at Cordoba, notably the provincial grenadiers commanded by Juan Maria de Morales. I undertook to carry this intelligence to the commanding general. It was close to 2.30pm that the bulk of the division came close to Cordoba. At our approach, the Spanish abandoned their position. Some retired precipitously, going round the town; others threw themselves into the town itself, where they barricaded the gates, either to defend themselves therein or to delay our advance. The commanding general demanded that the *corregidor* open the gates, assuring him that the inhabitants and their property would be respected. Any further resistance would be futile, since the town had no form of shelter from an assault, being defended by nothing more substantial than a wall in a poor state of repair and by a number of insurgents in full retreat. Already our young soldiers, animated by their first success, were showing themselves impatient to enter Cordoba in full force, despite the gates being closed. The order to blow them in with gunfire was duly given, and our troops launched themselves into the town at the charge. We found it deserted by the Spanish troops, who were fleeing in the greatest disorder, some along the road to Ecija, on the left bank of the Guadalquivir, and some through the mountains beyond Cordoba.

It became impossible, however, to restrain the greed of the soldiers, who, running through the streets with bayonets fixed, forced passage for themselves everywhere and spread throughout the houses in order to pillage. An early column, still marching in closed ranks, arrived in one part of town to be met by musketry from the windows in several streets; this fact led us inevitably to the conclusion that the inhabitants had taken up arms and were defending themselves. So a form of street-to-street combat broke out and served as a pretext for our soldiers to sack Cordoba and deliver it up to all the horrors of a town taken by storm. The soldiers scattered by platoons or singly, fully armed and unmoved by any representation made to them. Murder and pillage were soon joined by the rape of women, virgins and nuns, the theft of sacred vessels from the churches—

sacrilege accompanied by the most atrocious circumstances. Some officers—even some generals—demeaned themselves in indulging in such dishonour, even when grief-stricken parents sought to solicit the protection of the first officers they encountered. Happily for the name of French honour there were some sensible and generous souls who, in saving more than one family, protected them from the outrageous behaviour of a soldiery even more difficult to rein in once they had broken free of all the leashes of discipline. I had the good fortune to be able to save several women and some Spanish men who would otherwise have become victim of the soldiers' blind fury. Called to the aid of a woman in the greatest distress, I was forced to almost kill three frenzied members of a light battalion who, despite my efforts and the entreaties of the unfortunate woman, persisted in forcing their brutal attentions on her daughter, a charming young woman. Enraged, I struck the most impassioned of the three with my sword. He was about to be avenged by his comrades when, in order to avert a greater crime, I took up my pistols, threatening to shoot whoever dared approach me. Through such a steadfast attitude I imposed my will on these miserable creatures. I ran immediately to join other officers and we all retraced my steps and were able to save this unfortunate family, but unable to restore to them that precious honour they had lost. All kinds of disorder characterised this dreadful day and the scenes of desolation for which Cordoba provided the stage. The heat was so excessive and the soldiers so pressed by thirst that, without pausing to ask for drinks, they descended into the cellars and used their muskets to break open the great casks they found there in ranks, such that within a quarter of an hour they were swimming in wine and were drinking it without a break. By evening these same soldiers who had fought so well at daybreak could have been dispersed and overwhelmed by a thousand determined and well-led men. There, however, a benefit to the town in the outbreak of drunkenness that seized almost all the soldiers of the division; they soon succumbed to the inevitable need for rest and sleep, and this preserved Cordoba from a total sack—and perhaps its utter destruction.

Some inhabitants dared to venture out and made representations at our headquarters that it had been peasants and *montagnards* from elsewhere who had opened fire on the French troops and had forced the population of Cordoba into adopting a hostile disposition. Others stated they had only been prevented by the threats of terrible consequences by General Eschavari from opening the city gates and bringing the keys to General Dupont. It was, they said, solely these two reasons that had led to the calamities in Cordoba, which nobody was able to accuse us of anywhere else in Spain.

We could foresee the terrible consequences for our army, which would henceforth have a nation-wide war to undertake in the midst of an exasperated and unfettered population.

The following morning we were astonished to see General Dupont establishing the troops in camp, one part before Cordoba on the road to Seville, the other behind the town on the Madrid road.

The majority of the generals and officers, even the soldiers themselves, were expecting to continue the march on Cadiz. We could say, frankly, that the decision to remain static here in a rich town that had just been sacked was the cause of the loss of the army some six weeks later. There were really only two paths to follow: to march immediately on Cadiz, where we had inside sympathisers who, coupled with the terror of our force, would enable us to pass through the gates through a capitulation which would guarantee the inhabitants their possessions and wealth; or to march on Seville itself, home of an insurrection scarcely yet organised and where we could disperse the enemy's forces by means of rapid marches and well planned operations. But Cordoba became the Capua[18] of the Army of Andalusia, and by resting there it is tempting to believe that the principal reason for doing so was to protect the fruits of pillage rather than to seek out the enemy and bring him to battle.

What is certain is that a great deal of wealth was liberated there, not only from churches and private houses, but from the public treasuries also. There are several anecdotes that permit no doubt in this regard.

On the same day as Cordoba was taken, while pursuing the enemy close to the *porte de Seville*, an armed assembly

---

[18] *Translator's note:* This is probably a reference to the capitulation of Capua in central Italy on 28th July 1799.

was noticed off to the right; 50 grenadiers of the 4th *Légion*, commanded by *sous-lieutenant* Sablonnière, were sent in pursuit. The insurgents took refuge in the church and in the bishop's palace. After a lively exchange of fire, during which they suffered several dead and wounded, their leader, who seemed to be part of the bishop's entourage, offered to capitulate and further offered, if his life and that of his comrades would be spared, to indicate where the insurrection's pay-chest was hidden. Such magic words produced the desired effect. He was offered not only his life, but also protection. He immediately took *sous-lieutenant* Sablonnière to the place where the money was hidden in several chests, and assured him there was a total of 8-900,000 francs there, some in gold specie, some in silver. This officer made his report forthwith and Chief of Staff General Legendre ordered the chests to be seized and taken to him.

Major Teulet, commanding the 4th *Légion*, having been billeted in the house of the Provincial Receiver, found 1.2-1.5 million francs in gold and silver coin locked away there. He informed General Dupont, who ordered that the chests should be taken to the Chief of Staff. *Major* Teulet reported the quantity of cash he had found in his billet to his brigade commander, as well as the destination for it he had been given by General Dupont; he also reported the amount found by *sous-lieutenant* Sablonnière.

Other amounts were found in different locations, but positive information is lacking to be able to assess accurately the sums involved. Quartermasters were named to take inventory; these commissaries were the Chief of

Staff and his deputy, *commissaire de guerres* Lacombe, and *major* Teulet of the 4th *Légion*.

What a motive for staying in Cordoba! The soldiers themselves were not especially worried about staying there and during the first few days it was not easy to keep them in their various camps. But the officers, who could see the consequences of a war such as this, viewed the suspension of operations with regret. It was claimed that the Junta in Seville, far from being knocked back by the defeat of its troops, had just reorganised its army and given over command to General Castaños, and that the entire garrison of the camp at San Roque had augmented this army, which was already encamped at Ecija and Carmona, before Seville, waiting for General Castaños to advance once again on Cordoba. Besides these considerations, it was further suggested that it was prudent to await the arrival of the second division, commanded by General Vedel, before resuming the offensive. But all this intelligence on the threatening dispositions of the enemy didn't reach our headquarters till seven or eight hours after our entry into Cordoba. It became more and more dangerous to stay there and wait for the effect that the news of the sack of Cordoba, which spread everywhere so rapidly, produced throughout Andalusia and in the mountains of the Sierra Morena.

Exasperation was already at its height; reports coming into the headquarters from every quarter showed that officers and troops were being pitilessly massacred, if they travelled alone—even imperial couriers suffered this fate. The insurgents from the mountains were grouping themselves together in bands and descending on the hospitals, where they were cutting the throats of our sick and wounded; communications with Madrid could already be considered to have been cut; there was no longer any security en route, nor in the encampments or even in any post which was not supported by a body of troops capable of imposing its will on a furious but cowardly crowd, in which case we knew how to take it by the throat and master it.

We lost ten days in Cordoba waiting for reinforcements that were en route but which never arrived. There was no longer any hope of being able to subdue Seville, which had become the principal centre of the insurrection in Andalusia—an insurrection spread between the towns of Jaen, Grenada and even Cadiz, where an anti-French party had just been organised and had declared against the governor himself—General Solano, Marquis of El Socoro.

Emboldened by our inexplicable inaction, the Spanish advanced on Cordoba to resume the offensive, better commanded and supported by regular troops. Their generals and the Junta of Seville had spared no effort to exhort the mass of the populace. The check at Alcolea and the sack of Cordoba had been announced in the Seville papers, which lost little time in spreading the word to all Spaniards and even exaggerated the excesses and calamities accompanying the pillaging of Cordoba. They announced the city had been sacked for three consecutive days; that the churches, having been robbed of their ornaments and sacred vessels, had been converted into stables, and unfortunately these statements were true; finally they announced that a large number of the inhabitants had perished in defending their honour and the modesty of their wives and daughters against the brutality and arrogance of the frenetic soldiery.

One incident added not so much to the exasperation that was already growing among Andalusians as to the spirit their leaders had conceived to be able at least to chase the French army back beyond the Sierra Morena, if not to exterminate it completely. General Dupont had pushed forward several detachments beyond Cordoba on 13th June and three officers with around two hundred Swiss soldiers deserted to the Spanish advanced guard at Carmona. They gave as their opinion that Dupont's army contained two Swiss regiments formerly in service to the King of Spain and that they awaited only the right opportunity to turn their weapons on the common foe.

During the night of 15th/16th General Dupont learned from the *alcade* of Cordoba that General Castaños was advancing towards him at the head of a force amounting to at least 21,000 regular troops, 2,500 cavalry and substantial artillery, not counting the militia and volunteers who followed. As a result of a staff council attended by all his principal generals, he decided not to await the enemy at Cordoba, but to withdraw to the foot of the Sierra Morena via Andujar and Baílen. On the morning of the 16th, Dupont ordered camp to be struck and towards 7pm began a withdrawal that took on the resemblance of a full flight. Sat on a drum he watched the baggage train pass for five consecutive hours without taking any action to reduce its numbers or the embarrassment. Had the enemy been present the same day, the misfortune of 19th July would have taken place at the exit from Cordoba.

Everything we learned en route of the horrors committed by the insurgents against our isolated detachments adversely affected the morale of our soldiers and made a profound impression on them. We found recent and hideous evidence of the ferocity of our enemies.

For example, we had left a detachment in the village of Montoro to escort the bread produced by one of our bakeries. On the night of 5th/6th June, the baking of bread for the division having been finished, the detachment was busily employed in packing the bread while the local authorities were requisitioning vehicles to form a convoy. Towards the middle of the day on the 6th, the day before the affair at Alcolea and thus our entry into Cordoba—that is to say, before we had fired a single shot in Andalusia—the convoy set off, without drawing the least reaction on the part of the populace. Scarcely had they arrived on the main road when a group of some 7-800 locals assembled and, quickly moving by back roads known only to them, overtook the convoy and lay in ambush behind hedges. Unfortunately the detachment commander had marched off without taking any security measures at all—as if he were marching through the middle of France. Arriving at the ambush, he was surprised by the locals who leaped out quickly, fell upon the escort and massacred close to 200 French soldiers. A mere three or four managed to steal away from the fury of these wretched people, fleeing across country while the insurgents assuaged their rage on their unfortunate comrades. Arriving in Cordoba, they made their report; but were hardly believed, and it was not until we saw, during our return march, the corpses scattered on the road, or hung from trees, that we became convinced of the terrible fate of this detachment. We had the great sorrow to see several of our unfortunate soldiers on the road; one had had his arms cut off, another his legs; several had had their ears, eyes, nails and genitals removed. I myself saw one whom these tigers had crucified on a tree. He was terribly disfigured and presented such a hideous spectacle that I can still see this horrible scene today. I will pass over describing other refinements of this barbarism, which would serve no other purpose than to arouse a spirit of indignation.

Some distance from this location several of our soldiers, driven by thirst, had entered a house to demand something to drink; instead of finding the place inhabited, they had the misfortune to find the corpses of ten dragoons piled up one on the other, bearing all the marks attesting to how these poor unfortunates had suffered before dying. A little further on—around half a league from Montoro—we saw a sergeant of the 4th Legion on the side of the road with his feet and legs burned off up to the knee.

From that moment forward we trembled for the fate awaiting the wounded we had left at Cordoba, and we began to appreciate the calamities we should be preparing for and the extent to which our soldiers would undoubtedly take reprisal.

All of us at this point presumed the commanding general would take position at La Carolina—or, even more militarily intelligent, at Puerto del Rey. But on the 18th the corps took up position at Andujar. Subsequent to the

Marins de la Garde leaving this town, the inhabitants of Jaen had committed horrible excesses; they had brought themselves to Andujar en masse and had massacred the commandant and a weak guard we had left there to cover the hospital. Without the services of a lay priest who had no fear in standing up to the fuming mob, the wounded themselves and the wife of General Chabert as well as that of his *aide-de-camp*, who had remained at Andujar, would also have been massacred.

Forewarned of our return, the inhabitants of Andujar, certain of our vengeance, took heel for the mountains, taking with them everything they held precious and leaving the town without any supplies or resources.

The few inhabitants left were careful to make representations that the excesses had been committed by the insurgents from Jaen and those of their compatriots who, having joined the insurgents, had just fled. We contented ourselves solely with leaving the soldiers to spread out through the town to find supplies, rather than continuing our retreat to the foothills of the Sierra Morena to take command of the pass which led to Madrid, as the entire army believed. General Dupont took up positions at Andujar.

This position was in no way a military one and could not be considered as such by any definition. The Guadalquivir, fordable at every point during this season of the year, provided no decent defence. The position was even worse in that it was dominated by significant heights and, having no more than a single road by which we could

29

march to the Sierra Morena, left us vulnerable to having our retreat cut off.

Andujar had another grave drawback; as far as supplies were concerned, the town offered nothing. The scarcity was such that often we were able to provide only one loaf between sixteen men, with a little wheat to make soup, in place of vegetables; totally insufficient for our young soldiers, who were unable to procure any eau-de-vie, wine or vinegar. We thus saw the number of sick mount in a frightening manner; in less than a fortnight 600, almost all wracked with dysentery, filled the hospitals, not counting an equal number who, less seriously affected, remained in their billets.

General Dupont understood the need for supplies and, two days after our return to Andujar, put me in command of a detachment charged with searching Jaen itself for supplies and with punishing the town from which the swarms of brigands had come to massacre our troops. I set off on 20th June with a detachment of cavalry and the 3rd battalion of the 4th legion, a force that totalled some 5-600 men. I took care to advance with caution and to send out scouts along the line of march. A great silence took hold of the countryside at our approach. It was only as we approached Jaen that we encountered a body of rebels, but they were dispersed at the first charge and the first canon shot. It was impossible for me to hold back the soldiers, who were excited by the example of the sack of Cordoba and who knew, besides, that our mission was to punish Jaen and to locate supplies. The town was pillaged from doorstep to eaves for two hours and it was only through the most constant effort that I was able to prevent or stop a massacre. Happily, almost the entire population had taken to the hills. We went to a lot of trouble to form a convoy. I was intent this be carried out with the greatest alacrity, for fear my communications might be cut; but I was so on my guard that no body of insurgents dared to bar our passage. I returned to Andujar with the convoy intact and received from the commanding general the flattering statement that I had fulfilled my mission with as much intelligence as success.

Meanwhile, our couriers were being intercepted; all officers on assignments and all isolated soldiers were taken by bands of smugglers and peasants infesting the gorges of the Sierra Morena, where they found a dreadful fate. More than 400 sick left in the ambulances along the main road of Andalusia had had their throats cut in succession. The former Assistant Chief of Staff of the Army of Egypt, General Renée, newly arrived with General Dupont's corps, had just been burned alive close to La Carolina, as well as several other officers of the general staff.

There was concern in Madrid, where nothing had been heard from the Army of Andalusia for a month, since the couriers being sent by General Dupont were meeting the same fate as those from Madrid. It was at this moment that the Grand Duke of Berg, having heard nothing from General Dupont, ordered General Vedel, encamped at Toledo with the second division, to march off to reinforce the troops in Andalusia.

About this same time, General Dupont at Andujar finally received news from Madrid; he knew that the Grand Duke of Berg had fallen ill and had been provisionally replaced, as far as the direction of military operations was concerned, by General Savary, *aide-de-camp* to the Emperor. This officer wrote to Dupont that, on his own authority, he was sending assistance, viz: Vedel's division, which had received orders to proceed by forced march to the Sierra Morena, and two battalions that were already en route for the same destination. He also announced the imminent arrival of a convoy of flour and biscuit—urgent help indeed, since the troops at Andujar were already receiving no more than three or four ounces of bread per man.

On the arrival of these despatches, the commanding general again entrusted me with a command of around 1,000 men, with which I was charged with marching rapidly into the Sierra Morena, dispersing the rebels at La Carolina and facilitating the junction with General Vedel, who was en route with his division to cross the mountains. I marched immediately at the head of my column and, after having chased off the insurgents at La Carolina, established communication on 27th June with General Vedel who, the previous day, had opened the passes through the Sierra Morena in overthrowing an assembly of insurgents at Peña-Perros, where they had tried to block his passage. The road being opened up to his entire division, General Vedel, reinforced by my column, took position round the town of Baílen, having left in the Sierra sufficient troops to maintain communications with the province of La Mancha.

Meanwhile, after my departure from Jaen, the insurgents of the kingdom of Grenada had gathered there once more, in even greater numbers. In occupying this position, where they daily received reinforcements, they threatened our flanks and were positioned so as to be able to turn them via the gorges. Learning of this state of affairs, the commanding general wrote to General Vedel, directing him to send one of his brigades to Jaen, to chase off the Grenadans and to assemble another convoy of supplies, of which the army stood in ever greater need. General Vedel attached me to the brigade of General Cassagne, which was tasked with this operation. We left Baílen on 1st July and as soon as the next day we were before the town of Jaen. General Cassagne sought advice from me, since I knew the roads and the theatre of war. I had already indicated to him the precautions necessary to ensure we were not taken by surprise. Foreseeing also that, this time, we would encounter stronger resistance, I placed myself at the head of an elite advanced guard, having two field pieces that were soon employed against the enemy. We found them entrenched, having significant bodies of regular troops; but the greater part of their forces consisted of *montagnards* who had answered the call to arms. I immediately gave the signal to attack and, almost as soon as the Grenadans perceived we were about to turn their flank, they dispersed, leaving the road open. Only a few companies remained to engage us in musketry, as if to cover the retreat of the rest of their troops; but the regular troops resisted only briefly our several canon volleys and, after a brilliant action, we penetrated Jaen. I found the town deserted, entirely bare of supplies or any means of transport. General Cassagne having joined me, we established the position and, in order to fulfil the objective of our mission, decided to send detachments out in a one to two league radius around the town, in order to find forage and collect the livestock. The following day, 2nd July, at 5am, two such detachments having left, we were roused by the sound of musketry. We immediately beat to quarters, and with the whole brigade under arms, we were able to support the two detachments that were engaged with the enemy and were falling back on the town. We saw at once that we were dealing with an enemy even more numerous than we could have imagined. They were formed into three main bodies and were manoeuvring to surround us. During the day we lost about thirty soldiers. The following day, the enemy, having been even further reinforced, attacked us with renewed fury. All their efforts to overcome us proved futile, but we had cause to mourn the loss of Major Molard, commander of the 1st Legion. Persuaded finally that the objective of our mission was now unachievable, learning that the enemy was now very close and that we had absolutely no means of transport, General Cassagne ordered a retreat, which we carried out in good order. We hard scarcely left the town when we received a despatch from General Vedel who, informed of the state of affairs, recalled the brigade to his position. The enemy dared not follow us after the first league, and we rejoined our comrades at Baílen with greater glory than any real advantage. There is no doubt that these various combats served to instil confidence in our young soldiers, training and baptising them in fire.

In our conversations with several Spaniards, I detected a pronounced belief that seemed to spread throughout Andalusia, and indeed throughout Spain, that the French had begun to pillage Cordoba and the whole of this part of Andalusia without provocation and with no discernible motivation. This nation-wide belief was so deep-rooted that everything we could say to bring out the truth was to no pupose. From this situation stemmed the terrible reprisals to which we were exposed. From this perspective, the more I reflected on the consequences of the sack of Cordoba, the more I wished we had used other means to punish resistance in Spanish towns. In fact, if one examines every aspect of such an event, one must remain convinced that such a terrible abuse of power has even worse consequences for the army that perpetrates it than for the inhabitants who are its victims.

On 6th July I rejoined the headquarters at Andujar and I noticed with some chagrin that the commanding general had made no dispositions whatsoever, either for continuing the withdrawal or for a renewed advance. Cassagne's brigade, with which I had just conducted my second expedition to Jaen, had just been recalled by General Vedel and established at Mengibar. This position would have been preferable to that of Andujar, had it been occupied by the entire corps, since the insurgents would not have dared to attack such an advantageous position and success would have crowned any enterprise centred on this location.

But when the enemy had pushed his patrols as far as Mengibar, had established himself in force at Jaen and had occupied the position of Villa Nueva with a force of 8-

9,000 men, in a manner to be able to cut our communications between Baílen and Andujar—at this point all the principles of war forced on the commanding general the necessity of making a decision. Throughout history, indecision has proven to have the most fatal effect on armies. A decision—any decision—made and implemented firmly, is the only way to save armies in critical circumstances. An army divided into several detachments, each one of which finds itself too weak for the position it occupies, has no alternative before it but to effect a concentration.

Would the commanding general not reunite his corps at Jaen, or some other location close by? If, through instructions contrary to those of the Grand Duke of Berg, he found himself forced to maintain his presence in Andalusia, this position was without any doubt the closest to the mountains, the most advantageous and the one that offered the most resources of every kind.

I believe that I have been able to bring to the subject of this unfortunate campaign, better than anybody else, these general observations, based on events to which I was an eyewitness for the most part, and also informed by a knowledge of the theatre of war. It is true that I did not see everything; but coming and going between the headquarters of Dupont and Vedel, what I neither saw nor heard has been told to me by witnesses whose veracity cannot be called in question. Besides, I also had close relations with the main headquarters, established at Andujar, since the battalion of the *Marins de la Garde*, containing my comrades and my friends, had not left the area as I had, whether for Jaen, for Bailen or for La Carolina. It is precisely because I spent time in these different locations, and because I was in contact with general officers of the different parts of the corps, that all the circumstances of this campaign are known to me personally or have been related to me faithfully.

For greater clarity, I have combined here all the reports made to the main body commanded by Dupont at Andujar, which I had left there when I set off on my second expedition to Jaen—an expedition which I finished on 3rd July, just as I have noted above.

Let us first examine the defensive dispositions ordered by General Dupont. Colonel Dabadie, commander of the engineers, had erected a bridgehead on the left bank of the Guadalquivir, and these earthworks were manned by several companies of the *Garde de Paris* and by the 3rd Legion, under the command of General Pannetier. An ancient tower at the end of the bridge, which Colonel Dabadie had built into the earthworks, was occupied by a company of grenadiers. The various redoubts forming part of this defence were guarded by troops who were relived every twenty-four hours. But to build a bridgehead across a river which is fordable on both sides is not to offer a very formidable defence, above all when the sole point at which resistance can be offered to the enemy is dominated by hills, which were about to be occupied, earlier than we believed possible, by an already superior numbers of Spanish troops, to whom we had ceded the time to organise themselves. The commanding general could have avoided these disadvantages by deploying his troops on the right bank of the river in positions more favourable for defence.

The bridgehead and the various defensive earthworks would be completed by 18th July, a time when the division was feeling the disastrous effects of the dysentery caused by a lack of rations and by heat so excessive that ninety-year old locals had never seen its like.

But such was the poor state of our supplies that the soldiers found themselves forced to gather and mill the wheat themselves, at a mill where two companies of troops were forced daily to drive off the enemy in order to retain possession of this facility. In the hospital, already full to bursting, our sick had but a little wine and white bread, whereas the Spaniards before us were living in comparative luxury. Everything seemed to combine to overwhelm our soldiers. Although all these circumstances considerably reduced the effective number of combatants, the duties we had to perform didn't diminish in any way. The courage and resilience of the young soldiers made up for lack of numbers; every day we would send out exploratory patrols and, although these were little more than cautious, they were always pushed to the other side of the hills that dominated the camp and town of Andujar. The army, which had been about 15,000 strong when it left Madrid, had been cut in half by desertion, sickness and detachments. Two weak divisions had just crossed the Sierra Morena to reinforce the main body, but they remained several leagues distant and besides this, they had nothing of use to bring to the army in the form of sustenance and resources. A convoy of munitions and food had been taken close to Manzanarès and 150 cartloads of provisions had fallen into enemy hands. Our distress was at its height.

The division at Andujar already found itself in the direst military situation, without the possibility to sortie to march forward, unless considerably reinforced.

The enemy commander, Castaños, continued to advance along the left bank of the Guadalquivir and, advancing on Andujar, occupied the heights that are between this town and the village of Arjonilla. These troops were first seen by the two companies of *voltigeurs* of the *Garde de Paris* who every morning patrolled the crest of the heights dominating Andujar. The two companies had just arrived on the crest when they immediately saw a Spanish column, whose strength they estimated at 8-10,000 men, preceded by about 1,200 skirmishers. Our *voltigeurs*, numbering about 150, were joined by a company of grenadiers from the 3rd Legion and a detachment of thirty mounted dragoons. Despite the enormous numerical superiority of the enemy, this small force awaited the enemy at the halt, in order to give the commanding general time to take appropriate action, the commander of the patrol having immediately sent him a despatch rider to alert him of the Spanish movement. But it was impossible to resist 1,200 skirmishers for long, 600 of whom marched in close columns towards our centre, while some 400 were spread out in order to turn our flanks, supported by 200 regular cavalry, who could cut off our retreat if the detachment were unnecessarily to be obliged to defend a position that was the objective of an entire army. The enemy established itself on the heights that same morning, and its batteries being completed by evening, it became master of the plain and forced us to take cover on the other side of the river. The first brigade of Barbou's division lined up to left and right of the bridge, and General Chabert, at the head of the second brigade, was extended to the right and formed the first line of defence. Dupont had placed the Swiss brigade in reserve, under the orders of Generals Schramm and Rouyer. General Frésia, at the head of the cavalry, formed up in the plain behind the town, sending scouting detachments along the course of the Guadalquivir. Finally, on the northern side, 7-800 men under the command of General Lefranc guarded the foot of the hills dominating Andujar.

These dispositions having been made, General Dupont sent an officer of the General Staff, one Desfontaines, to General Vedel at Baílen, in order to warn him of the movement of the Spanish and to request of him one of his brigades to reinforce the troops defending Andujar. The next day, the 16th, the Spanish directed a lively cannonade against the redoubt and the flanks of the bridge, where they noticed one of our battalions drawn up. Our redoubt responded feebly to the enemy fire since, our communications with Madrid having been cut, we were being miserly with our ammunition, trying to reserve them for more decisive actions. Despite the ferocity of the enemy fire, we suffered but ten or twelve killed and wounded, since most of the shot hit the shoulders of the earthworks or were lost in the river.

On this same day, 16th July, while General Vedel was on route from Baílen to join the commanding general at

Andujar, a column of 10-12,000 of the enemy, commanded by Don Theodore Redding, attacked General Liger-Belair at Mengibar, forced the ford across the Guadalquivir and, overthrowing two French battalions, took command of the position. General Gobert having advanced with two battalions and a regiment of cuirassiers to support General Belair, the fight broke out again between Baílen and the Guadalquivir. Several charges by the *cuirassiers* at first halted the Spaniards, but their infantry having been reinforced, a prolonged fusillade broke out along the length of the line. A musket ball hit General Gobert in the head and he died the following day of his wounds. His death reduced our troops enthusiasm and General Dufour, who had replaced him in command, led them back to Baílen to cover this important position. But under the false impression that the enemy was manoeuvring on his right in order to turn his flank by the Bazea road, he abandoned this position and marched on to La Carolina, wishing thus to prevent the enemy cutting the corps' communications with Madrid.

At midday, the first column of Vedel's division, having left Baílen, came within sight of Andujar just at the moment that General Castaños was prosecuting a new attack. One of these columns, about 5-6,000 strong, came down the hill and seemed about to force the passage above the town. But Castaños, informed of the arrival of reinforcements, broke off the attack and took off in a new direction, as if to move towards Mengibar in going upriver once again.

Perhaps this was the moment to take the offensive with the two newly reunited divisions and, taking advantage of the division of the enemy forces, throw back on Cordoba or Mantilla the forces before Andujar and follow that by bringing to battle those forces before Bailen. But the commanding general seemed preoccupied with nothing other than remaining at Andujar and, separating General Vedel once again, sent him off in the direction of Bailen to push back the enemy who had taken over this critical position at the mouth of the gorges between La Mancha and Andalusia.

General Vedel, leaving Andujar at 5pm the same day, arrived at Bailen the following morning, 17th July. Finding General Dufour no longer there, he followed the latter's march to La Carolina, having orders to join him and believing, as did Dufour, that the enemy occupied the gorges in order to cut the army's communications and that it was imperative at all costs to hold these positions open.

Thus, through a series of false impressions and unfortunate circumstances, the forces of the commanding general, amounting to a total effective force of 22,800 men, including 3,700 cavalry and 38 canon, found themselves dispersed whilst, had they been centralised, they could have overthrown all before them.

However, General Castaños, who had been informed during the night of 16th/17th of the departure of Vedel's division for Bailen, assembled a council of war on the morning of the 17th, at which it was concluded that the division of the Marquis de Coupigny would combine with that of General Redding and that the two would jointly attack Baílen, while the enemy's third division and reserve, under the direct orders of General Castaños, would divert the attention of the French with a diversionary attack on Andujar.

On the 17th the Spaniards debouched onto the plain of Andujar some 15-20,000 strong, with the intention of launching a diversionary frontal attack while one of their columns would make for the point at which the river was fordable. General Dupont's forces not being sufficient to man the entire line, the French generals took care to place their troops wherever they were necessary, by which means they fatigued the enemy who, still masters of the heights, from which they could discern our movements, directed upon us an extremely lively cannonade. The fire from our redoubt on this day ceded nothing to the enemy. It was just so well directed that the majority of our rounds struck the enemy masses, which finally decided, around 3.30pm, to return to the hills. Our losses were barely noticeable—those of the Spanish remain unknown, due to the distance at which they were drawn up, enabling them to shelter from the cannonade and being exposed solely to our shot and our howitzers.

The movement of Vedel's division almost as soon as it had arrived led us to hope that during the same night we would be able to commence our retreat towards Madrid, or at least that we would be able to effect our concentration in the gorges through the Sierra Morena, where the strong positions would enable us to prevent the Spanish army from reaching La Mancha. There we would be able to resupply ourselves and would be much more easily in communication with Madrid. Actually, as early as the 17th Dupont had ordered the camp at Andujar to be struck, but by an inconceivable error, this was delayed until the 18th.

However, the commanding general was certain that the enemy, from the position at Villa Nueva, was already manoeuvring in his rear. On the same day of 17th July, a battalion of the 4th Legion, sent by Dupont to the Rumblar bridge, had been unable to establish itself there and had instead taken up post between the bridge and Andujar. The definitive order to strike camp was not given till 8pm. Our dispositions were such that any kind of success became not only unlikely but also impossible. We had to impose our will on the enemy, but by virtue of the order of march one can be easily convinced that such an objective could never have been achieved. The following details of the order of march on the night of 18th/19th July will clearly demonstrate this assertion. A battalion of the 4th Legion, the grenadier and *voltigeur* companies of the other two battalions of the same legion, two 4-pounders and a squadron of chasseurs formed the advanced guard, which left at 6.30pm for Baílen. The rest of the troops left camp at 8pm in the following order.

Two battalions of the 4th Legion (from which the grenadier and *voltigeur* companies had been drawn for the advanced guard) moved off first, with four cannon; then came the baggage train, which occupied an enormous length of road, escorted by men drawn from each unit and by the third battalion of the 4th Swiss, part of Chabert's brigade—a total of 2,200-2,300 bayonets. The remaining troops followed the baggage train and consisted of the 'Spanish' Swiss regiments Preux and Redding, some 1,400 strong and commanded by the two generals we have already identified.

Following on were two battalions of the 3rd Legion and two battalions of the Garde de Paris, constituting Pannetier's brigade, about 2,200-2,300 strong. Then two regiments of *chasseurs à cheval*, less the squadron allocated to the advanced guard—a little over 300 sabres in total. Then a company of light artillery—about 50-60 men. The whole of this brigade fell under the orders of General Dupré. The troops bringing up the rear consisted of two regiments of dragoons—about 300 sabres and a squadron of *cuirassiers* about 75 strong, commanded by General Privé. Bringing up the rear was the battalion of the *Marins de la Garde*, about 250 strong and finally some 250 pioneers.

By virtue of this order of march, there were some 2,000 men marching ahead of the baggage train and more than 5,000 following it. This sequence would have been appropriate if one had nothing to fear from the enemy except from the rear but, with certain information to the contrary—such that the commanding general could not possibly doubt it—perhaps he hoped to hide his march from Castaños at Andujar? And yet this entire deployment was evidently contrary to the principles of war.

At daybreak, the advanced guard arrived on the plain at Rumblar but, instead of finding a French division there, as our troops expected, they found the outposts of the enemy, who repulsed them. Here is what had taken place at Bailen. When General Redding had dislodged General Gobert's forces from the positions it had occupied in the neighbourhood of Baílen, he fell back on Mengibar, re-crossed the Guadalquivir and the same evening took up a position in which he could be joined by the Marquis de Coupigny's division. During the night of 17th/18th the combined struck camp and moved together on Baílen to attack the French. General Redding entered the town at 9am on 18th and discovered that the French had fallen back towards La Carolina. He immediately established outposts in the direction of Andujar. One can discern here that had it not been for the unfortunate 24-hour delay in the commanding general striking camp, he would have been able to occupy the critical position at Baílen in advance of the enemy. This failure now led to an inevitable retreat. Not only were the two divisions of Redding and de Coupigny united at Baílen, but the enemy reserve, commanded by Lieutenant-General La Peña, was now marching in the same direction. All that remained at Andujar was the main body of the army under the orders of General Castaños and this would indubitably be following our small army which would inevitably be caught between two forces.

We thus found the forces of General Redding three quarters of a league from Baílen, occupying the heights, crowned with olive trees, which dominated the small bridge across the Rumblar. Six battalions were placed in echelon and defended the defile through which we must pass, about three quarters of a league in length. These various positions, covered with olive groves, led to the small plain at Baílen, occupied by Redding and de

Coupigny's troops drawn up in battle array in three lines and covered by a strong battery established on the only road along which we would have to pass on emerging from the trees. Such was the position in which we now found ourselves.

The enemy's advantages were substantial and they would be able to dispute the ground yard by yard with troops who were malnourished, exhausted and fatigued, who had been marching since 8pm in terrible heat, ravaged by hunger and thirst, not even having had the time to quench their thirst at the Rumblar bridge nor to rest even five or six minutes to catch their breath.

It was close to 3am when the first canon fire from both sides announced a decisive action. Our advanced guard was brought to battle to the left of the road and its two 4-pounders were almost immediately dismounted from their carriages. General Chabert having requested reinforcements, the commanding general gave the order to advance to two battalions of the 4th Legion, its accompanying artillery and Dupré's brigade. The *chasseurs* and the artillery arrived well before the infantry battalions which, had their advance not been delayed by the baggage train, would have been but a half hour distant from the advanced guard and could have joined them within an hour: instead they took at least two hours. The advanced guard had suffered significantly since they arrived and were now extremely fatigued. However, this small reinforcement placed General Chabert in a position to take the offensive. After significant efforts we were able to take the enemy's positions in the woods and to push back their battalions, which fell back on their main line of battle. It was not yet 5am when we came out onto the plain before Baílen, but as soon as our canon were deployed in batteries, they were destroyed.

To the 2,000 men forming our advanced guard now were joined the 2nd battalion of the 4th Swiss—the last unit of General Chabert's brigade. It was 9am by the time that the regiments of Preux and Redding arrived, followed a brief while later by General Privé's brigade.

Battle was now joined at every point of the line. We sought to face up to every movement of the enemy, whose numbers so exceeded ours. We hoped to find a gap in the line, or at least to bring the enemy to a halt, just until the arrival of General Vedel who, we were told, was just four leagues from the battlefield. We tried several attacks on different parts of the enemy line, and took advantage of the ability to form up our columns hidden from the enemy's fire, as a result of the heights we had seized. But we were truly exhausted, and were continually marching from one place to another. The various units of our cavalry made superb charges, which would have resulted in taking the enemy's principal artillery battery if the infantry had been able to follow. Each unit had taken an enemy flag during the heat of the action. A Spanish regiment had been overcome by 100 *cuirassiers* of the 5th Regiment commanded by *capitaine* Verneret; they had traversed the Spanish lines three times.

Both armies had equal motivation for making extraordinary efforts. Our motivation was simply to pass through and to force the position; the Spanish objective was to hold firm. Each army was threatened with being caught between two forces; we, by the principal Spanish force that we had left behind on the heights of Andujar during our retreat and which could, as a consequence, arrive in our rear at any minute; and General Redding by the arrival of General Vedel, who had set off from La Carolina and therefore could not be too far from the battlefield.

Thus, from their reciprocal positions, the two armies were under equal pressure to bring to a head an action that needed to be concluded and that would effectively seal the fate of one of them and, without a doubt, the future independence of the Spanish nation, for nothing speaks quite so loud in political affairs as an initial victory or an initial defeat.

But enormous mistakes characterised our manoeuvres. Pannetier's brigade could not occupy its position before 10am. This last reinforcement was composed of troops whose approach march had been so rapid that they arrived totally breathless. The baggage train had held them up. They could do nothing but form themselves up and be immediately thrown into disorder.

The enemy's artillery was of heavier calibre than ours, which would have produced an entirely different result had we been able to employ it in concentrated manner. But we never had more than four pieces in battery—and frequently less.

It cannot be doubted that, had the commanding general left the baggage train at the end of the column of march, instead of placing the bulk of his forces behind the train, and that, instead of allowing the gradual arrival of units, 7,000 bayonets could have been advanced against the enemy as one, in battalion columns, then the passage would have been forced and our own troops would have become masters of the field of Baílen before 6am. They had nothing to fear from La Pena's peasants, who had been left in front of Andujar—our troops' movement had given them a nine-hour start on this body. There were also Castaños' troops, who could not arrive in sufficient time to take part in the action. There was a further obstacle in front of them—one for which they had limited solutions—how to cross the Rumblar bridge. The banks of this small river are steep and the river itself is full of enormous blocks, rocks and stones. Passage of the enemy artillery would be impossible until they had retaken the bridge; infantry and cavalry would be unable to cross the river except with the greatest difficulty, and we had left a battalion of the *Garde de Paris* to guard the bridge, under the orders of General Barbou. Also there, in position on the heights that dominate the Rumblar, to defend the position against those troops who might follow us from Andujar, was Barbou's second brigade, with the battalion of *Marins de la Garde* also placed in reserve. Thus it can be seen that initial errors were compounded by others, and that the measures undertaken and the dispositions effected did not conform to the principles of the art of war.

Our troops, brought to a halt by the whole enemy line, tried once more to renew their attacks. The task of the cavalry was even more difficult, since they had to manoeuvre on ground cut up by ravines and planted with olive trees. General Redding, reinforced by the forces of the Marquis de Coupigny, began to extend his front further and further in order to outflank us on the right. He threatened to attack us there at the same time with two battalions, which had just manned the crest of a high hill. Two new charges, prosecuted blow for blow by General Privé, achieved only minor advantages, without being able to dent the enemy line, which had become more and more compact. In vain the commanding general paraded before us the Spanish colours that had just been taken by Verneret's squadron of *cuirassiers*, by *sous-lieutenant* Castait of the same unit. The two flags were greeted, it's true, by cries of *vive l'empereur!* But that was the limit of the ardour and the enthusiasm of our troops. They were exhausted from fatigue and devastated by the heat. Their starvation was so great that, no longer able to support their arms, they threw them to the ground and waited where they were without moving. The battle had been going on since 3am and already half the day was spent. There simply was no spirit left for another bayonet charge—this had already been tried three times without success. Only the intrepid *Marins de la Garde* demonstrated a resolve that none could overcome. The commanding general, seeing no sign of the arrival of Vedel's division, losing faith in the ability to break the enemy's strong line—which was formed of his best regular troops—and having also been informed of the impending arrival of Lieutenant-General La Peña's advanced guard on the field, despaired of the day. The defection of part of the Swiss troops rattled his morale. The Swiss brigade, whom we had taken up from Spanish service, passed over to the

Spanish side almost in its entirety, despite everything Generals Rouyer and Schramm did to try to prevent them. The latter general was wounded and the fatal example of this defection won over even the Swiss battalion of Colonel Freuler. More than a third of our line troops were now *hors de combat*. In such a dire situation, the commanding general—already vanquished, one might say, by the general despondency as much as by the strong resistance of the enemy—resolved to enter into discussions to arrange a ceasefire.

General Dupont had on his staff an *officier d'ordonnance*,[19] M. de Villoutreys, who was also an equerry to Napoleon. It was he who had brought despatches from Madrid and it was he the commanding general chose to parley with the enemy commander and arrange a cease-fire. M. de Villoutreys left between 4 and 5 o'clock and arrived at the outposts of Lieutenant-General La Peña, from there being conducted to Major General Redding who, having heard his initial submission, stated his conviction that the commander of the French army must surrender unconditionally. Villoutreys observed that he had no other instruction but to negotiate a ceasefire, or perhaps a capitulation with the objective of persuading General Castaños that the French army should pass through Baílen to re-enter the province of La Mancha. General Redding agreed only to a provisional ceasefire and referred General

---

[19] *Translator's note*: Often translated as 'orderly officer', but this carries slightly different connotations in modern English and I have therefore elected to keep the French designation.

Dupont's request to General Castaños. No aspect of the ceasefire was agreed in writing and no demand was made for inclusion of any unit but Barbou's division, which alone had fought this day.

Meanwhile the divisions of Vedel and Dufour, having left La Carolina during the course of events, were moving towards Baîlen. They halted at Guarroman, where General Vedel allowed his troops to rest and refresh themselves. Towards 5 o clock—almost the same moment at which the ceasefire had been agreed—Vedel's division arrived in the rear of General Redding's forces. This latter officer immediately sent two representatives to inform General Vedel of the conclusion of an armistice. Vedel sent his *aide-de-camp* Meunier off to verify this and, not seeing him return within the time he had specified, moved in to attack the enemy.

Taking advantage of the suspension of hostilities, I took myself off from the army headquarters to that of General Vedel, who had just arrived in the enemy's rear, where I saw that he had set his troops in motion for an attack. I had no details of the armistice and believed it applied to all divisions of the army. I therefore approached the Colonel of a Spanish regiment, whose troops were lying on the ground, their arms stacked, and who had just received orders to stand to. I managed to persuade him to prevent his soldiers from opening fire and to observe the suspension of hostilities currently in force between the two armies. But General Vedel continued his activities and 1,500 enemy soldiers were taken prisoner, together with two cannon and two colours. I confess that I then believed the ceasefire had been no more than a ruse on the part of the commanding general in order to gain time for the arrival of General Vedel, and I rejoiced inwardly at a circumstance that would allow us to extricate ourselves from our dire situation. Indeed, General Vedel was pressing home his advantage and catching General Redding between two forces when Barbarin—General Dupont's *aide-de-camp*—arrived in the middle of the fire fight, carrying a verbal order for General Vedel to initiate no new action against the enemy and to await fresh orders. General Vedel obeyed this order and so disposed his troops. He was entirely ignorant of the situation of General Dupont and his forces, of which he learned only the following morning, on the belated return of his *aide-de-camp*, Meunier.

Meanwhile General Dupont received a communication from General Redding, complaining that he had been attacked during the truce, contrary to the laws of war, by General Vedel, coming from La Carolina with reinforcements, and that the Cordoba battalion had been surprised and made prisoner with two field pieces. He requested and even demanded that the artillery and all the prisoners be returned to him. General Dupont accordingly sent a written order to General Vedel, instructing him to return the prisoners and canon to General Redding, which angered the entire division and caused General Vedel himself to share bitter observations with me. He could not conceive what possessed General Dupont to act thus, at the very moment that he received reinforcements offering him the opportunity to change his fate. It was at the end of this conversation that he begged me to go and propose to the commanding general an attack on the enemy from both sides the following day, 21st, at daybreak, on an agreed signal.

I arrived at headquarters, which I found in a state of confusion. I could see that negotiations were in progress, but I was not allowed into the conference area. I managed only a brief interview with the commanding general, and we discussed means of attacking the enemy. General Dupont appeared beaten and discouraged to me. I also believe, according to what one of his *aides-de-camp* told me, that he was suffering from dysentery which, coupled with the wound he had received during the battle and the unhappy outcome of the previous day's affair, weakened his morale and robbed him of the energy necessary to achieve an equable result. He was thoroughly imbued with the impossibility of achieving a happy outcome and threw himself back instead on the principal conditions of the truce already agreed with the enemy. I know not whether this treaty had already been signed. What I do know is that I received no notification or communication whatsoever—I am merely stating here what little positive information I learned regarding the circumstances surrounding the capitulation. I can state categorically here that General Privé did suggest to General Dupont a similar stratagem to that which General Vedel had charged me with conveying. He suggested that there still remained a method of forcing a passage, that all was not yet lost and that it would be necessary to sacrifice the baggage train, currently guarded by 1,500 elite troops who would thus become available. He also suggested that in concentrating all the infantry against the enemy's right wing and flanking his left with the cavalry, it would be possible to successfully push in the enemy line and pass the initiative to General Vedel. Finally, he suggested that the preparations for this attack would be simple and that the state of the terrain would prevent the Spanish from observing the formation of our columns. General Dupont remained absorbed in difficult reflection on this desperate but potentially successful plan. I am justified in believing, however, that General Privé's suggestion preceded mine and in fact was made at the moment that General Vedel's arrival first became noticeable.

As for the capitulation, I know that the equerry Villoutreys had been sent to General Castaños to obtain passage for General Dupont's army under the conditions already agreed, and that he had returned to announce that General Castaños demanded the army surrender unconditionally. A Spanish orderly officer arrived to present a similar summation. The commanding general, having assembled a staff council, turned to General Marescot, who had no position with the army but had been charged on the Emperor's behalf with inspecting the coastline at Cadiz. He asked Marescot to find Castaños, whom he had known in the Army of the Pyrenees in 1795 and with whom he had maintained cordial relations, and to intervene and obtain the requested capitulation, that is to say the safe conduct of the troops in retreat for Madrid.

General Marescot, having left to confer with Castaños, came across General La Peña, whom he had also known in 1795, at the head of the Spanish advanced guard. This officer announced that he was empowered to negotiate, but demanded that all French troops—including the divisions of Dufour and Vedel—should surrender unconditionally. General Marescot protested at the severity of this position and General La Peña therefore consented to view only Barbou's division as being prisoners of war—the other two divisions would have merely to evacuate Spain by sea, having their weapons returned to them prior to embarking. The general committed himself to obtaining the agreement of the English. General Marescot forwarded these proposals to the commanding general, who assembled his council of war immediately, and developed the plan to accept and sign the articles of capitulation.

I did not await the return of General Marescot before setting off to report to General Vedel the failure of my mission. I told him that I had no firm information regarding the details of the capitulation, but that I had heard tell that his division were not prisoners of war. I added that the commanding general advised him to withdraw towards the Sierra Morena. General Vedel immediately commenced such a movement, but scarcely had he set off when an *aide-de-camp* arrived with a counter-order. At first he took no notice and continued his march as far as Santa Helena, where he arrived at midnight on 21st. There he received a definitive order to cease his withdrawal and remain where he was—he also learned that his division was now included in the terms of the capitulation.

In fact, the Spanish generals had refused to compromise, at least as far as General Vedel's division not being included in the negotiations was concerned, and when he began his withdrawal they exploded into reproache and accused General Dupont of perfidy. Considering the state of affairs as they were, this motivation was more than sufficient for General Dupont to employ all the means at his disposal to ensure General Vedel's division was included in the negotiations.

However, nothing had yet been definitively agreed— neither the respective positions nor the duration of the armistice had been formally defined. General Castaños, in bringing up all his troops, was compressing and surrounding Barbou's division further and further.

At the same time Generals Redding and Castaños detached the Marquis de Coupigny's division to take possession right away of the gorges in the Sierra Morena and to cut all communications with those divisions not already encircled—and to follow their movements.

General Dupont, unhappy with a negotiation that hitherto had been limited to representatives, gave over his powers to General Chabert, but without any written instructions. He contented himself with telling Chabert to insist on obtaining an evacuation to Madrid via Baílen. Villoutreys and General Marescot agreed to accompany General Chabert, without being included in his negotiating powers, but also with verbal instructions. The negotiations were opened on 21st July at the post house between Baílen and Andujar, where the French negotiators found the Conde de Tilly, commissioner extraordinary from the Supreme Junta in Seville, who presumed to join the negotiations in his capacity as representative of the insurrectional government. Our generals at first demanded that the army be allowed to withdraw towards Madrid and further undertook these troops would take no further action against Spanish forces. Perhaps they would have obtained such an agreement had it not been for an incident that countered the goodwill General Castaños bore towards General Marescot. An enemy unit had intercepted a despatch from General Savary to General Dupont, informing the latter that serious developments in Old Castille and Galicia necessitated the immediate return of Dupont's troops to Madrid, in order to concentrate with the main body of French forces. This unfortunate news having made an impression on the negotiators, a capitulation which made all the army's troops prisoners of war was drawn up, communicated to the commanding general, consented to by him, concluded and signed on 22nd July by General Chabert as authorised representative and by General Marescot as witness only. The document stipulated most particularly that the baggage train would remain unharmed—especially the baggage of the generals. In the opinion of the entire army, the baggage train contained, at least in part, the spoils of the sack of Cordoba.

The army awaited its fate as spelled out by the capitulation. It had been acknowledged, during the cease-fire, that the Spanish generals would provide us with food, of which we were entirely devoid, to the point at which our soldiers were collapsing from exhaustion and starvation. It was not until 23rd July that Barbou's division received any viands, with the result that our poor soldiers were exposed in the olive groves for four days to the heat of the sun without bread or food of any description.

On 24th July we paraded before the enemy army with full military honours and we then laid down our arms. It is impossible for me, even after several years, to recollect these events without a pang in my heart. We were all saddened and in despair, not understanding how we had been led into such a humiliation. The capitulation itself was bad enough—the bad faith we experienced in such a piteous manner of avoiding execution was almost more so.

General Marescot, not being part of the army's organisation, was returned to France via Seville. Villoutreys, the Emperor's equerry, who had exercised great influence on the negotiations and had discussed and agreed the articles of the treaty which brought reproach down on the heads of all those who had been a part of it, was returned to Madrid with a Spanish escort, and from there he returned to France via Bordeaux.

Our army of prisoners marched off on 24th July, in two columns, for the ports of Rota and San Lucar, where it was to be embarked. I was in the first column with the *Marins de la Garde*, the *Garde de Paris* and the 3rd Legion, as well as the headquarters troops. Under the terms of the convention we had retained our swords. A Spanish line regiment was charged with escorting this first column, which began the army's progress. According to the capitulation, it was to be embarked for France at the ports of Cadiz, Rota, Porte-Sainte-Marie and San-Lucar de Barameda. The 2nd and 3rd divisions marched on Malaga and neighbouring small ports, to be returned to France with their arms, artillery and baggage. We rested on that first day at Villanueva. The second day was somewhat stormy. Arriving at Bougaleure, we found some 1,200 militia who were resolved to join with the inhabitants and cut our throats while we slept. Informed in time of this dastardly plot, the commanding general solicited the Spanish colonel commanding the escort to allow us to bivouac in a neighbouring meadow, to which the colonel consented. As soon as they had eaten, the soldiers left their lodgings and gathered in the meadow, to the obvious great discontent of the militia and inhabitants. They were furious but, even armed as they were, they dared not come to execute their plan in the meadow. With some pushing and shoving, we left Bougaleure relatively quietly. On 26th July we broke our journey at Castro-del-Rio, on 27th at Rumblar and on 28th we arrived in the charming village of Ecija on the bewitching banks of the Guadalquivir. There, beneath a magnificent sky, we were subjected to every sort of humiliation on the bridge at Ecija. Women spat in our faces—we trembled with outrage, but the slightest demonstration of indignation would have caused our deaths. Such a humiliating reception determined the commanding general to request that we be bivouacked on the public promenades rather than in lodgings in town. Dictated by forewarning and sagacity, this action saved us. Despite all our precautions, several of our soldiers were killed with stilettos. General Pannetier's secretary, among others, was gravely wounded towards 9.30pm, some five or six paces from our bivouac.

On 29th July we spent the night at Fuente, on 30th at Las-Real, 31st at Ultrera and 1st August at Hascabeza.

On 2nd August we arrived at Lebriga, where we remained till the 12th. During our stay there, General Chabert was sent to Seville, so as to be informed of the anticipated date of our embarkation for France. But the Spanish had already violated the capitulation, with the greatest lack of fairness. The Junta of Seville first adopted the pretext that they were awaiting passports from the English Admiralty, in order to ensure the safe conduct of our troops to France. But the Admiralty, in agreement with the Junta, having refused to issue the passports required, the latter body hesitated not at all to reveal its true nature. The commanding general sent justifiable complaints in vain to General Morlat, Governor of Cadiz, regarding the tardiness in carrying out the terms of the capitulation. On 10th August he received the following letter.

> "*Dear General Dupont,*
>
> *I have never acted either in bad faith or in falsehood; from this basis stems that which I have communicated to Your Excellency on 8th inst., written with great candour, as is my practice, and I am saddened to find myself obliged by your response of yesterday's date to repeat in brief that which I have already had the honour to communicate to Your Excellency, and which can certainly be verified.*
>
> *Neither the capitulation, nor the approval of the Junta, nor even an express order from our beloved sovereign can make possible that*

which is not possible. There are no ships for the transport of your army, and no means of procuring them. What greater proof of this can there be than we have held here the prisoners from your naval squadron at enormous expense, without the means to transport them elsewhere, beyond the continent? When General Castaños undertook to request from the English passports for your army, he did not undertake to do any other thing he was entreated to, and that is what he has done. But how can Your Excellency believe that the British government would agree to allow you safe conduct, when it is certain your force would again make war on them in a different place, or perhaps in the same place?

I am persuaded that neither General Castaños nor Your Excellency believed other than that the terms of the capitulation could be executed. The objective of the former was to escape embarrassment, and that of Your Excellency to obtain conditions that, although impossible to meet, made an honourable surrender possible. Each of you achieved what you desired, and it is now necessary that the imperative law of necessity should operate.

Our national character does not permit us to exercise it with the French except according to this law, and will certainly not allow of reprisals. Your Excellency forces me to express to him those truths that will distress him. What right do you have to demand the execution of an

*impossible capitulation concluded with an
army which entered Spain under the veil of an
intimate alliance and union, which has
imprisoned our King and Royal Family, sacked
its palaces, murdered and violated its
population, destroyed its fields and seized its
crown? If Your Excellency does not wish to
experience the ever-increasing justifiable
indignation of the people, which I am trying
hard to suppress, he should desist from the
similar and increasingly intolerable complaints
and should seek, through his conduct and
acceptance, to dull the strong feelings brought
on by the horrors he recently committed at
Cordoba. Your Excellency should rest assured
that my objective in offering him this advice has
no other end but his wellbeing. The irrational
general populace believe only in repaying ill
with ill, with no appreciation of circumstances,
and I am unable to prevent myself holding
Your Excellency responsible for the dire
consequences that may result from his loathing
for that which must be.*

*The arrangements that I have instructed
Don Juan Creagh to make, and of which I have
informed Your Excellency, are those authorised
by the Supreme Junta and are, moreover,
indispensable in the current circumstances.
The delay in their execution is alarming the
populace and attracting disadvantageous
attention. Already the aforementioned Creagh
has acquainted me with a fact that causes me
the gravest concern. What an irritation it must*

*be for the populace to learn that a single soldier
carries 2,180 livres tournois![20]*

*This is all I have to say in response to Your
Excellency's despatch, and I trust that this will
be the last communication on these subjects,
whilst I remain, in all other matters, desirous of
being agreeable, your admiring and sincere
servant."*

This letter amply demonstrated that we remained
prisoner and that only the general staff would be allowed to
return to France. We were, in fact, now directed towards
Cadiz and arrived at the port of Santa Maria on 14th August,
from which we would continue to Cadiz, where we were to
be embarked and transported to France. The baggage train
preceded us with a Spanish escort, though this consisted
only of the baggage carts of the general officers—no
soldiers' wagons formed any part of this train. The carriage
and wagons of the commanding general and his chief of
staff were in the van, followed by those of the divisional
and then the brigade commanders. A search, in which we
took no part, having been started on the right of the train,
revealed church silver in the first wagons examined. On
seeing this, the searchers and the local population, who
were already agitated and milling about, cried out that here
were the spoils of the sack of Cordoba. We arrived at their
location, hoping to calm the assembled multitude, but we

---

[20] *Translator's note:* the *livre tournoi* was a currency previously
used in France, named after the town of Tours, where it was
minted. It was abolished during the French Revolution and was
replaced on 27th March 1803 by the franc.

found the people seized by fury and the majority of the generals and staff officers were cruelly mistreated and robbed of their baggage. It was impossible to contain the populace, who were already trying to seize hold of us. They threw themselves at our baggage with furious energy, exclaiming that they would at least deprive us of our spoils. Without the arrival of a considerable armed force and the intervention of the senior officers, we should have been massacred.

The commanding general wrote immediately to the Governor of Cadiz, demanding the return of those possessions of which he claimed to have been robbed. General Morlat responded the same day in a letter even more imperious than the first, and of which the following are the principal passages.

> ".....Certainly it was never my intention,
> nor that of the Supreme Junta, that Your
> Excellency and your army should be allowed to
> remove from Spain the spoils of your pillaging,
> your cruelty and your sacrilege. Do you believe
> us to be entirely stupid and insensible? Can a
> capitulation that stipulates nothing regarding
> security except for the baggage be used to
> protect booty obtained by the violence, murder
> and desecration of every description that took
> place in Cordoba and other towns? Are there
> laws, reasons or principles that can prescribe
> the faithful observance or even exercise of
> humanity towards an army that enters a
> country as friend and ally, under false and
> deceptive pretexts—that has treacherously

exercised its power against an innocent and well beloved King and his Royal Family, and is then believed to have authorised the sacking of the nation's palaces, the desecration and robbery of its churches, the murder of its ministers and others—that has oppressed the people, stolen everything that could be moved and destroyed that which could not? Is it possible that such men, when deprived of the terrible fruits of their iniquity, dare invoke the principles of probity and honour?

Perhaps you wish to propose that I myself should rob and pillage the churches of Cadiz in order to restore to you that which the populace has removed from that which you yourself have stolen with so much desecration from the churches of Cordoba? Your Excellency should not allow himself such illusions and should instead content himself that the nobility of character of the Spanish people will never permit them to be cast in the role of butcher."

It is with regret that I must describe such documents, without which my narrative would be incomplete. Doubtless it required nothing less than such a violent crisis for a general officer to allow himself thus to address an imprisoned and unfortunate general, and to add such reproaches without offering the least positive proof. One must beware of rushing to judgement based on malicious protestations or on simple presumptions, and in preparing material for historical use we should protect ourselves against all forms of partiality and against all surprises.

The entire staff of General Dupont and the other leaders of the army—with the exception of the general officers of Vedel's division, who had already been dispersed throughout Andalusia—were transferred to the fort of San Sebastian in Cadiz, along with a certain number of senior officers, including myself, and various functionaries of the military administration. During the first days of September we were embarked, in order to be returned to France, via Marseilles, where we arrived after an uneventful and monotonous voyage.

It is well known that the Emperor ordered the arrest of Generals Dupont, Vedel and Marescot on their arrival. I thought for a moment that I would share in their disgrace, in part if not in whole. But the Emperor recalled that he had promoted me to the rank of *capitaine de vaisseau* as reward for the success of my two expeditions in Andalusia and he knew, as well, that I was entirely uninvolved in the capitulation at Bailen and Andujar. Nevertheless, at first he welcomed me coldly, but several days later, having summoned me into his office and having posed several questions on the unfortunate close to this campaign, he said to me, on the subject of General Dupont: "What I can never forgive him for is having parleyed with rebels; even had he parleyed with but an English sergeant, I could have let him go."

EPILOGUE

The rest of the life of the courageous Pierre Baste is less known to us, the additional papers and notes of which we have knowledge not going any further. Nevertheless we do know quite positively that in 1809 he took part in the campaign in Austria; that he fitted out a flotilla on the Danube and that, charged with seizing the island of Mulheiten, he carried out his orders with as much audacity as celerity. The enemy having been forced to abandon this island, Baste's success facilitated the French army's passage of several branches of the river and prepared the way for the memorable battle of Wagram. In addition, as early as 15th August Napoleon raised him to the rank of *comte*, conferred upon him an annuity of 20,000 francs and named him *colonel* of the *Marins de la Garde Impériale*.

After the Peace of Vienna, inaction could not satisfy him and he took himself off anew to Spain, where he was named commander of the flotilla at Boulogne, commandant in the *Légion d'Honneur* and finally Commodore. At the beginning of 1813, the Emperor gave him a particular task. He was to go to Swedish Pomerania, where he was to serve under the orders of General Morand and, as commander of the fleet, to take all necessary measures for the defence of the island of Rugen and the coastline. He was also to visit the mouth of the Oder in order to give the appropriate orders, dependent on the circumstances. But on 20th March, Napoleon decided the mission of Commodore Baste would not be undertaken and on 21st December in the same year he named him *général de brigade* in the army. It was in this role that he was killed, in February 1814, at the battle of Brienne, at the age of 46.

Baste cut a dashing figure. He had a brusque tone and the manner of a sailor who knew how to combine kindness and severity with a fierce demeanour. He was courageous to the point of foolhardiness.

He had served in twenty-five campaigns in the eastern and western colonies, on the coast of Africa and in the Ile-de-France. He had taken part in fifteen actions, in the siege of Malta and in various actions with the fleet at Boulogne. He had been commander of seven different ships of the fleet, had commanded the crew of the *Marins de la Garde* and, in this role, had been involved in the campaigns in Germany and Spain. At the end, he met a glorious death in defence of his nation.

Lightning Source UK Ltd.
Milton Keynes UK
21 March 2011

169614UK00004B/9/P